ALCHEMY
of ABUNDANCE

RICK JAROW, PH.D.

ALCHEMY of ABUNDANCE

Using the Energy of Desire to Manifest Your Highest Vision, Power, and Purpose

SOUNDS TRUE

Music by Dawn Avery

Cover art by Richard Borge, www.richardborge.com

Published 2005

Printed in Korea

ISBN: 1-59179-287-8

Library of Congress Control Number: 2005927087

Other audio learning programs by Rick Jarow available through Sounds True:

The Beginner's Guide to Finding Your Perfect Job, CD

Opening to Shakti, cassette

The Ultimate Anti-Career Guide, cassette, CD

The Yoga of Work, cassette, CD

For Maika, whose play lifts my heart——may the radiant bliss of existence always flow through your dance!

Thanks to members of the Advanced Manifestation Program in New York, whose intent and energy helped birth this volume; to Tami Simon, Randy Roark, and Sounds True for believing in my work and taking the time to work it out; to Sheri Bresson for her editorial support and expertise; and to all the unseen ones who guide me in grace.

TABLE OF CONTENTS

Introduction to the Art of Manifestation

A NUMBER OF YEARS ago, in a dream, I found myself on a long search with two elders, one on each side of me. We had been seeking the "crown jewels" and had entered a deep cavern where I discovered a large pool filled with clear golden ghee—the clarified butter used for ritual offerings in classical India. I knelt down and peered into the pool, and there I saw the jewels, shimmering under the surface. I reached down with trembling excitement, when suddenly the elders on each side simultaneously ordered me to stop. They informed me that these were not the jewels we needed and that I had to return to my own land and engage in contemplative prayer.

This "big dream," as C.G. Jung might have labeled it, became a call to the Alchemy of Abundance, directing me—after years of travel and study in Europe, India, and the Middle East, after initiations and long terms of practice in various yogic and healing traditions, and after years of intellectual pursuits in the philosophy and aesthetics of religion—to return home. "Home," not just in the sense of returning to the roots of Western tradition (after all, the three of us were enacting the search of the Magi for the Christ), but a return to the heart of prayer and to the soil, the *humus* (from where the word "humility" comes from), to my world of the Hudson Valley and to a spiritual path that would be non-different from everyday life.

Yet, when we turn toward home, we hold all the energies of all the places we have been. We weave them back into the tapestry of our experience and they enrich our communities and ourselves in a new way. This program, then, is the fruit of years of work and an ever-deepening intuition that our unique place in time demands a unique vision: one that integrates the great insights and traditions from all times and places with the here and now. To put it simply, no major world religion was ever founded in or upon a democracy, and the rise of the individual and the great American experiment of the pursuit of happiness—predicated upon the freedom of conscience—demands that each of us walk the earth in our own way. This is true abundance: to cower before no one and no thing, to honor the life we have been given, and to dare to open to our fullness. At the same time, we are asked to walk together, to open to one another with our compassion, and to perceive and create forms of connection that keep us related without sacrificing the freedom we have gained at such great cost.

If abundance honors the dignity, goodness, and value of the individual, then alchemy—as one of the great disciplines at the root of Western culture—honors the collective. I use "alchemy" here, not in the sense of some arcane esoteric lore, but in the way that Jung, Hillman, and other depth psychologists have construed it: that the journey of purifying base metal into gold is an inner one, organically ordered by the wisdom of the psyche through its unfolding in the life of the individual.

I am using "alchemy" then to denote an inherent and authentic process of self-realization present in our cultural milieu, one that need not be imposed upon a person, but rather one that unfolds through the interaction of inner imagery and outer experience, the fruit of which is pure living wisdom, the "philosopher's stone." The hermetic, alchemical teachings, in fact, offer us the richest body of spiritual practice to have been developed in the West, and we owe our modern interest in depth psychology and astrology to them. Moreover, they are our own equivalent to the *Tantric* traditions of the East as the Tibetan Buddhist teacher Chögyam Trungpa Rinpoche once remarked, calling Alchemy "the *Tantra* of the West." Indeed, the practice of Abundance may itself be a part of the evolution of our own Tantric tradition: one that does not get caught up in organizations but that honors the soil upon which we stand, the unique situation of every person, and the mysterious fusion of opposites—masculine and feminine, compassion and wisdom—as the core of the "Great Work."

The modern Alchemist may not be holed up in a laboratory, but he or she understands that the true field of experimentation, the *alembic,* or vessel, where the work is done is within the self, and that the "self" is not some abstract entity above and beyond the world, but is squarely within the world—within everything and everyone. Enlightenment, then, is not conceived of as an "ultimate state" but as the ongoing reality of this moment: the intersection of time and timeless that obliterates neither, but opens to a rich panoramic vista of teeming life as divinity itself: the ongoing experience of abundance.

This program is about realizing this abundance in our lives. It is about creating pathways to participate fully and consciously in the "Great Work" of alchemical transformation. Through the guided explorations and working with the zodiacal mandala, you will witness the ongoing fusion of dreams and archetypes with the most ordinary and practical of situations. You will understand and experience your own unique ability to generate well-being in every aspect of your life and to share it with others.

The core practice here, akin to the alchemical distillation of gold, is known as "manifestation," bringing the deepest, purist expression of your life into visible form. As with Tantra, there is an understanding that all that is necessary to realize your full potential is already present. You are simply asked to deal consciously with everything that is happening in your life as your practice of abundance, wholeheartedly and nonjudgmentally. As you will see in this program, by learning to trust the flow of creativity that naturally moves through your life, you will forge profound connections with everything and everyone in your world; you will come home to the humus, the soil, of your own daily life, and discover a level of abundance that has always been and ever-will sustain you.

Very often, when people hear about "abundance" and "manifestation," they think about getting what they want, and what they want is magic and miracles. One challenge in the *Alchemy of Abundance* is to accept and work with the very earthy reality of particular situations. Patience, perseverance, and persistence are the key qualities that can help move you from dreaming into action. When things are cramped and difficult, when it looks like you cannot make it through, the techniques in the *Alchemy of Abundance* can inspire you to focus and move forward. The proper respect for your current reality will lead you to accept situations and see them through to completion. When you have fully grounded yourself in reality, mastered the techniques and explorations included in this program, and learned how underlying forces bring things about, you will then be able to experience and express what to others will seem like magic and miracles.

In this program, you will become familiar with powerful processes that can be mastered, and with subtle energies that can be harnessed, to achieve what you most want in your life; this is the "alchemy" of it. These forces are real, and their power is palpable. To be a contemporary alchemist is to work clearly, honorably, and consciously with them, leaving no stone unturned. The ongoing use of the guided meditations on the CD included in this program will allow you to perceive your current situation in its contemplative depth and beauty. The visualizations are designed to take you deeper into your own being, allowing you to uncover and examine the vast array of profound forces operating in your life as you begin to hear the music of the spheres in the walk-a-day world.

In the spirit of the great hermetic and alchemical traditions, we will be working with a mandala that includes twelve realms, patterned after the signs and houses of the zodiac, which are the backbone of the hermetic structure and language. Each of these realms is a doorway through which you can explore specific areas of your life, to clarify and empower what you want to bring into being. The process of working with this meditational model is to learn to move into each of the mandala's realms effortlessly and repeatedly and to then return to your center, incorporating the visions and information you have received. This interweaving will allow you to integrate seemingly separate perceptions and experiences into a vision of your life in which everything is seen as part of a greater whole. It is this interweaving process of exterior and interior, self and other, immediate and universal, that is "Tantric" (from the verb *-tan,* "to weave") and that will reveal the integral tapestry created by the various facets of your experience allowing you to bring it all back home.

The real work of manifestation is to weave these strands of your life into a "Temple of Beauty" that can sustain you beyond ego-based narratives of dominance and survival and beyond romantic fantasies of lack and longing. It is about learning to trust the practice of opening yourself, heart-first, to all of existence and letting your experience of who you are, what you are doing, and where you are going expand into its natural flowering.

By creating your own Mandala of Manifestation, you will literally transform your fate, bringing disparate aspects of your life experience into relationship and, hence, into a more controlled focus. Instead of being unconsciously caught in the patterns of your life, you will become a conscious and active participant in the process of manifestation that is available to you in every moment. You will see classical mythology unfolding in your daily life as you discover your own artistry, building your mandala as a daily practice. You will find yourself more deeply engaged with the natural elements, the cycles of the seasons, and with others around you as you realize what riches exist and have always existed right here, in your day-to-day life, which is the realm of abundance.

CHAPTER
ONE

What Is Abundance?

BEFORE WE BEGIN to discuss abundance, let us be clear about what it is not. Abundance is not the result of a Faustian pact to achieve personal greatness. Such quests are, in fact, often motivated by feelings of inadequacy. Abundance is also not about running around and trying to score as many points as possible before the game ends. It is not a race to see how much you can get done in a week, or in an ambitious five-year plan. Abundance is not about the accumulation of goods; nor is it the unrealistic renunciation of material comforts. Neither is abundance about finding a way to remain merely comfortable—a safe way to stay lukewarm.

In essence, true abundance is freedom. It is fundamental well-being, a fulfillment that is not dependent on exterior conditions. Abundance is learning to trust life. It is reality lived fully—being conscious, present, and whole.

Therefore, the *quality of your attention* is the genuine measure of abundance, and it is your greatest capital asset in any situation.

What we come to understand and affirm is that even through the most difficult circumstances of life, abundant beauty and richness may be found. It is our faith in the goodness and wisdom of things that allows us to work our way through life's darkest moments. In this way, abundance is also faith in the basic goodness of life. It is saying "yes" to all that we can know of life—including the suffering that surrounds us. It is also saying "yes" to that which we do not know, to open and accept the unknown with grace. A sense of abundance gives us the freedom to participate fully in our lives by doing what we can to assist others. If we do not ourselves feel rich, how can we give to others what has been given to us? In this way, abundance becomes the rainbow shining through the storm, the promise of our divine destiny.

The practices included in the *Alchemy of Abundance* will help you through challenging times by giving you concrete tools to deepen your faith, your patience, your generosity, and your power to realize that what you desire in your life is the abundance of beauty and blessedness that always abounds in the present moment.

In Indian tantra, such practice is known as *sadhana*, a term that indicates the pursuit and practice of virtue and its power. The word comes from the Sanskrit verbal root *-sid*, which means to straighten, to get straight, to get clear, and to bring things into alignment. The Tantric yoga of manifestation is thus a constant "straightening"—aligning our will with the will of the universe and our desires with the reality of the moment. What is unique to the alchemical approach of manifestation is that this "straightening" is not only moral but aesthetic as well. One without the other would certainly be limited. If we solely try to be good and moral, we often become dry and lifeless, and if we only focus on beauty or on what is emotionally powerful, we risk becoming sentimental or shallow. The alchemical path of manifestation involves the integration of our moral fiber and ethics along with our aesthetic and magical sensibility.

Before we can begin to explore the Alchemy of Abundance, we must answer some fundamental questions. First, we must ask, "Why do anything? Why bother even getting up in the morning?" Or as my son used to say to me when I would ask him to make his bed, "Why should I make my bed if it's just going to get unmade again?" In short, we are asked to confront the issue of desire, its reality, its fulfillment, and its frustrations in the face of an impermanent world.

In the Western alchemical tradition, the instinctual level of desire is envisioned in terms of the *Uroboros*, the great serpent endlessly devouring its own tail. Here, the Uroboros is a symbol of the incessant cycle of desire motivated by ignorance, with only a spark of consciousness. At this level, making things and doing things perpetuate ignorance, and there are many examples of neurotic manifestation: the blind piling up of objects and information, the corporate encouragement of mindless consumption, the power of attention siphoned off through television and other media. The inevitable frustration of such desire leads to either nihilism and despair, or else to spiritual fantasies of an "afterlife" that keep one from being engaged here and now. Within the urge of desire, however, is also the urge for illumination. And so the question becomes how are we going to act?

The celebrated Hindu scripture, the *Bhagavad Gita*, emphatically tells us that we act because we are obliged to—that we are literally moved into motion by enormous forces: by hunger, desire, by the weather, by the dynamic powers of nature. Seen in this light, our wanting demands an ongoing engagement with the realities of our existence. Our choice is not whether or not to want or to do, but how to want and how to do in the face of what is.

Some time ago, I was pushing my daughter on the swings in a park at twilight by the Hudson River. As I was looking past the river at the mountains of New Paltz, the river and the mountains suddenly transformed into the Ganges as it flows through Rishikesh in India. At the same time, I remained conscious that I was by the Hudson River bank while pushing my daughter on the swing. I knew that before my daughter was born, I had been in Rishikesh, and I sensed that a time would come when I would be back in Rishikesh. Perhaps I would wonder if any of this had actually happened, and yet it was happening. In that moment, I experienced an overwhelming and powerful opening into the great gift of being in front of the river, at that moment, pushing my daughter on the swings, *because* I knew it would not last forever. It was something akin to what the Japanese call *mano-no aware*, the deep sadness of life that opens into an appreciation of the beauty and love in a fragile and impermanent moment. The sadness of that moment was that someday my daughter would be too big for me to push on the swings, and that some day—all too soon—there would be no more swings and no more playground and we would both be in other places. But it was that fact that made that moment all the more precious.

Manifestation in this sense has to do with opening to the wisdom and destiny of our desire, with allowing circumstances to come into existence as well as with releasing them when it is time to let them go. Therefore, the work of manifestation is an art, but it is a very different type of "art-work" than that of producing objects or manipulating circumstances.

The process of manifestation is one of opening up to the preciousness of every moment and responding to it creatively. In this way it may be thought of as a compliment to mindfulness. We know that the bed will become unmade. We know that someday we will eventually die, but in this moment we are asked to participate fully in the process of creation, sustenance, and dissolution, all of which is part of manifestation, the art of full, participatory living.

Such full, participatory living can lift us out of the dilemma of Sisyphus, who endlessly pushes a rock uphill, only to have it roll down again. The process of manifestation will allow us to take whatever situations we have been given, imbibe them fully by releasing habitual judgments about their value, and then make the best design we can out of them as an offering and appreciation for being fully alive.

The work of manifestation is also more than a personal question of who we are and what we want to do. In order to accomplish anything, we need to be in living exchange with others, as clearly as we are dependent on so many people when we sit down to a meal—including the farmers, the cooks, and the servers. Our exchange with others, therefore, is crucial to our life's work of manifestation, and this sense of exchange, of sharing, of giving and receiving, is one of the fundamental reasons for our desire to manifest in the world. By becoming conscious of the relational aspect of manifestation, we go beyond egocentric desire and experience the desire to increase our possibilities for love, and for awakening the experience of joy in our connection with others.

What does abundance look and feel like to you? Buy a journal or notebook and have your answer to this question be its first entry—articulate what well-being feels like and how its manifestation would look like for you. Is it living at a certain level of passion and joy? Is it a particular type of employment, a lifestyle, an environment? Does your vision include family members and friends? Allow your imagination to run free. Include visions in as many different areas of your life as possible—financial, material, professional, personal, social, familial, global, and spiritual—but always proceed from the visceral feeling level of abundance. Then make your list as long and as detailed as you can, continuing to add to your list as you move through this program.

CHAPTER
TWO

Gateways to the Temple of Beauty

GRATITUDE

A sense of gratefulness for the gift of life is more than mere sentiment. When you allow gratitude to flow into your heart, you naturally want to give back, and all good things begin to naturally unfold.

One practical way you can begin to manifest an attitude of gratitude is to pay attention to all of the service people in your life: the people who drive your buses and taxis, who give you tokens at the train station, who cook your food, deliver your mail, and clean your clothes. Whenever you go to the store, a restaurant, or connect with service workers, allow yourself to appreciate the gift they are giving you. After all, without the people involved in producing this book, you would not be able to read it. Without the farmer, the truck driver, and the store clerk, you would not be able to eat. When you become aware of how your happiness and even your survival relies on the services of thousands of people you may never meet, you will begin to feel a sense of appreciation for the talents, abilities, and contributions of others. When you have developed this sense of appreciation, you will experience a much stronger and easier flow with the world around you—not only in your business, but in your own home as well.

What are you grateful for? Try to bring to mind all of those who have inspired you throughout your life and the members of your current community. As you continue through this program, try to become aware of everything that supports you in your practice of the art of manifestation, especially those moments when you experience a heightened sense of gratitude.

CONFIDENCE

Confidence is the cornerstone of personal power, and people who exude confidence can persuade almost anyone of anything. But what I am talking about here is not manufactured confidence, or confidence even in yourself necessarily, but a greater sense of confidence in the process of life, as well as confidence in the importance of your life and your contributions. Such confidence often supplies the energy that you need during difficult times in order to keep going forward and accomplish your goals. If you do not have confidence in yourself or your projects, you will more easily give up when things become difficult.

If you have confidence in life, you will be better able to envision your place in it and express it to others clearly, and, when you meet resistance or things get difficult, you will have enough security in the underlying principles of natural abundance to see what changes are necessary in order to come into alignment with your greater vision. In every life, there will be times when everything seems to happen effortlessly, and there will be times when you seem to be blocked no matter what you try to do. Developing a sense of confidence allows you to recognize your place in any situation according to the present flow of energy. Sometimes this requires you to take a more active part in the process, and sometimes it demands that you take a more passive role.

I heard of a man who was wanted by the Gestapo during World War II. He had been hiding in a hotel in Vienna when the Nazis, searching for him, entered the hotel. At first he looked for places to hide in closets, under beds, etc. But realizing that there was no place to hide, he took a deep breath, filled himself with confidence, and put on his best clothes. Then, without hesitation, he went down through the lobby and walked out the front door!

The next time you have any doubts about what to do, remember this. Do not hide, do not panic. Take a deep breath, open to your full confidence, and allow yourself to walk through the world in your power.

Recognizing the quality of moments as they are happening, and what response they are asking of you, is one of the most important tools for increasing your ability to manifest whatever you desire. Moreover, learning to recognize, appreciate, and reinforce those times when everything seems to be going your way can give you the support and encouragement you need to maintain your confidence even when things do not seem to be going your way.

When have you felt that everything was going your way? Where were you? With whom? And what were you doing? Allow yourself to fully feel that moment, as if you were there again, as if you are there now. If the energy of that time could guide you today, what would it ask you to do? Where would it ask you to go? And who would it ask you to be with? In what ways do you feel confident in your life; in your path? What is actually working for you currently, and how might these things expand in the coming weeks? Note how this type of confidence work is diametrically different from processes that begin with focusing on what is wrong with you. Let abundance become your cornerstone, and the building will follow in kind. As you continue with this program, try to become aware of those moments when you feel deep confidence in the process of life itself despite its difficulties.

ALIGNMENT

Once you recognize and become familiar with the feeling qualities of ease and appreciation that occur at times when your desire and the universal flow seem to be one and the same, you naturally want to know how to maintain this space. The way you do this is to bring yourself into alignment with what is actually happening in this moment. This is known as being "in the right place at the right time," and this can serve as our working definition of "alignment." When you are sensitive to the importance of being in the right place at the right time, you naturally gravitate toward areas where you are most effective, and when you are struggling, this helps you realize that there is not something wrong with you or your vision, but rather that you are not in the right place to take advantage of your idea's power and usefulness.

Acting out of a sense of scarcity and panic often leads to being in the wrong place at the wrong time. In such situations, your attention is often on what you want to get out of a situation, which is a backdoor way of focusing on where you are in lack. When you are operating out of abundance, you are drawn into situations not for any petty personal reasons, but because they feel right—for yourself and everybody else. But if you repeatedly find yourself in situations where you are not getting what you need, it is important to investigate why. In terms of the science of manifestation, sometimes you will find yourself in a job or in a certain situation because you need to learn something quite specific. Therefore, before you make judgments about unpleasant or difficult circumstances, ask yourself, "What do I need to learn in this situation?" In this way, you learn how to navigate through challenging circumstances rather than abandoning them. In fact, many people find themselves repeating the same types of dissatisfying situations until they learn how to befriend and work with them. Perhaps the most pointed practice I have heard of in this regard was that of one of my mentors, Hilda Charlton, going to a psychic in Santa Barbara (named Mrs. Perkins) every week for the simple fact that she did not like her. Hilda intuitively knew that, as long as she held her resistance, she would keep running into "Mrs. Perkins" wherever she went. She kept going until her reactions were gone, and then she was free. This is a very "Tantric sadhana," a fierce practice, because instead of just coasting through paths of least resistance, you challenge yourself, you put your base metals in the furnace so that they may become purified gold.

There are other situations where what you are asked to understand is that what used to be of value to you is no longer a part of your path. When you do not realize that a particular path is no longer of use to you, you may think that you can make it right solely through an exercise of will, and thus find yourself in familiar situations two, three, or more times before accepting that you no longer belong there. In situations like this, "no" is often the correct answer.

The main characteristic of proper alignment is an experience of effortless flow—things seem to naturally and easily come to completion. You have a sense of watching things happen on their own without needing a great deal of energy or manipulative force. However, our life experience is often one of misalignment. Instead of effortless flow, we experience frustration, difficulty, rejection, and failure. A habitual response to this is to get angry and blame others, "the market," or the current social or cultural situation. Instead of looking at ourselves, we see the world as out of alignment with our great idea, or we create major dramas about how unfairly we have been treated. When I used to visit my mentor Swami Jnanananda Giri in the Himalayas, I would bring him "news of the world," often accompanied by a litany of complaints. To this he would respond rhetorically, "Are you in the world, or is the world in you?"

The practice of abundance responds "Yes" to both. You are in the world and the world is in you. You work with the world in such a way that you can acknowledge its misalignment and respond compassionately, as you simultaneously allow it to open you to your own conflict and woundedness. Then, when you sense yourself out of step with things, you can remember that difficulties and detours offer profound gifts. The degree to which you become aware of how and where you are experiencing "dis-ease" is the degree to which you will be able to move into deeper alignment—not getting locked into judgments, and thus using your situation as a means to open your heart and mind.

There will rarely be sustained periods of complete and total alignment. Once you are at a certain level of graceful and effortless flow, new challenges surface from the shadows, or you experience parts of the world that are not on your wavelength, or you draw in other people and work with their misalignments, all as part of your own process.

As you develop a solid foundation of gratitude and confidence, you will find yourself worrying less about your particular role in a situation and instead become aware of what you are being asked to do in any given moment. Sometimes the way you find your next step is by simply paying attention to what people are asking you to do. It does not mean that you have to accept the requests, but you can sift through them to identify what has been genuinely calling to you.

✻

List all of the situations you can remember where you felt yourself in harmony with everything and everyone, in the right place at the right time. Allow yourself to honor those moments of alignment by reliving them, and by acknowledging what they gave to you. How might these situations expand and evolve at this time? In future time? As you continue with this program, try to become aware and enter into those moments when you feel yourself to be in the right place at the right time.

MENTORSHIP AND TRADITION

When you pay attention to the messages that surround you and how they often mirror your own internal needs, you will become aware of the importance of being among the right people and situations. Therefore, a significant step in this part of the process is to find others who have been successful in what you desire to create. If you can find a lineage or a tradition that you resonate with—one that has ideals, goals, and visions that are congruent with your own—you can find the nourishment and confidence that will help you to accomplish your goals and see them in a larger context. When Bob Dylan was a young man, for example, he heard something in the songs of Woody Guthrie that inspired him to leave home and move to New York City in order to follow that line. If he solely wanted to have a successful music career at that time—in the early 1960s—he would probably have gravitated toward the Brill Building, or any of the other "popular music factories" of the time. There was very little market-ability for someone in their early twenties singing blues and folk music with an acoustic guitar and a harmonica. Still, Dylan felt an overpowering attraction to the dust bowl songs of Woody Guthrie, and even dressed like him and began singing in Guthrie's style. But he also learned from everyone in that tradition, borrowing songs and melodies and the finger picking styles of his elders and making them his own. By finding so much outside of himself that he could appropriate for his own uses, he did not have to create everything out of whole cloth, and this "borrowing" was a means to nourish himself while building the base of knowledge and self-confidence that he would need in order to take this tradition and transform it in his own particular way.

To begin this process of finding your place in a lineage, you need to ask yourself what traditions call out to you. In what situations do you feel most comfortable, interested, and valued? Who do you genuinely admire and understand as a possible model for your own life? Once you become aware of your answers to these basic questions, you often do not need to go out and find a particular person or tradition, but instead you can open up the antenna of your attention and become aware that you naturally resonate with certain people, teachings, and places. To find yourself in these kinds of situations is not a chore, but rather one of the greatest pleasures in life because you will experience your own desires and energies resonating with those around you and will be able to receive and understand their energy and guidance as part of your own authentic and creative way. It is often in situations such as these that we first understand how effortlessly everything happens when we are in the right place at the right time.

It is important to remember that this connection you feel with another person or particular way of life is something that is intended to bring out your uniqueness, and it never amounts to slavish imitation that reduces or restricts your genuine feelings and abilities. Just because you have found someone who can serve as a model for your own life path, and who speaks to you, does not mean that you necessarily agree with everything they do or say, or that you agree with how they behave in every situation. In fact, a very important part of apprenticeship is to recognize and honor how your own path differs from that of your mentors.

Draw a map of your own lineage of inspiration. Who inspired you when you were ten, fifteen, twenty, and so on? Who have you consciously or unconsciously chosen to model in your life? Who would you like to move closer to? Who do you know who has skills or the energy that you would like to possess on your path? In what ways might you bring those people more strongly into your sphere of attention?

WALKING EYE-DEEP IN HELL

The Alchemy of Abundance includes learning how to live with—and accept—not realizing your goals, along with the frustration and sense of failure that may accompany such experiences. This part of the path of manifestation is what the poet Ezra Pound described as "walking eye-deep in hell." "Eye-deep" because instead of resisting it, you allow yourself to remain awake even at the bottom of confusion and despair. What you will find is that when you accept that the worst has already happened, all of the energy that you have been using to resist or deny this possibility suddenly becomes accessible to you. To open to what we have been afraid of releases powerful healing energy and makes it much easier to know what is necessary in order to bring yourself back into alignment. Sometimes you can only see all the possible resolutions and available options when your back is up against the wall.

But since these moments are some of the most stressful in the process of manifestation, it is important to learn a few techniques for how best to deal with them. The first thing you need to do when you find yourself in a difficult situation is to allow yourself to feel it fully. Whatever you are most afraid of in the present moment, breathe it in completely. If you get a bad review at work, if someone said something that really hurt you, if your loan application was rejected by the bank, if you were passed over for a promotion or failed to get a job your really wanted, breathe it in completely, and realize that even so, it is still alright because you are alright in terms of your fundamental, basic sense of well-being.

When you have arrived at a place where you can accept failure, rejection, and disappointment completely and release reactive judgments, you have completed a cycle of manifestation. You have traveled from a conscious attitude of gratitude for what is here already, to developing personal confidence, to coming into alignment with the process, to finding mentors to deepen and expand your vision, and opening yourself to be able to deal with whatever the universe has put in front of you. Then, when you go forward again, you will be stronger and clearer. Instead of losing energy condemning yourself or others, you have walked eye-deep, you have experienced and known, and such awareness is invaluable. Cycles will continue to repeat in your life, and instead of carrying resentments, your skills will deepen and your understanding will evolve—until any terrain you walk on becomes a practice of deepened participation with everything and everyone, which is the root from which powerful manifestation will arise.

❦

Make a list of all of the times you have felt yourself eye-deep in hell, and what lessons you have learned in those moments. What insights and skills have been born in you from these moments? What unexpected gifts have you been given in these difficult situations? Allow yourself to fully receive their lessons, despite whatever negative associations these memories might bring to mind. If you do this seriously, you will begin to let go of any ideas about being "a loser" or "a failure" as you perceive and acknowledge these gifts and your newfound strengths. As you continue with this program, whenever you hit a pocket of failure or disappointment, allow yourself to open further to the lesson you are receiving by asking yourself where this situation wants you to go, what it wants you to do, and how it wants to deepen you and make you more compassionate and whole.

THE YIN WILL AND THE YANG WILL

Chinese medicine speaks of the yang will and the yin will. The yang will is about wanting: the furnace that one needs in order to make things happen. The yin will, on the other hand, is about peace of mind: a deep appreciation for the intelligence of everything exactly as it is—a notion that things can always work out on their own.

When the yang will is operating at a low level, it behaves like the Uroboros, filling time with cycles of desire and activity that never fully satisfy and have very little value. People who operate solely via the yang will tend to race through the day, struggling to get as much accomplished as possible, believing that "time is money." But the yang will can also create real value in our lives. It allows us to set goals and meet them, to finish projects, and overcome adversity.

When the yin will is aligned, it is like a deep reservoir—when it is open and flowing, things naturally come to you. But the art of manifestation is not solely about getting what you want. A lot of people get what they want, but remain chronically dissatisfied because they have not aligned their wanting with the true fullness of their being. In fact, if you feel content that you are getting exactly what you want in life, it is probably because you are thinking too small.

When the yin will is operating at a low level, you do not have the energy or desire to make anything happen. You develop philosophies of fear because you do not feel at home or fully alive, and it is difficult to generate enough energy to follow through or finish your projects: you never write the letter, you never make the phone call, you never answer the email, until it is too late. An imbalanced yin will, then, correlates with the fear of moving into action, a fear of getting up and accomplishing something.

The middle way here is to steer through both excessive activity and inertia, and to allow the way things are to support your striving. Such action opens effortlessly into greater and greater appreciation and awareness. The practitioner of the Alchemy of Abundance finds a way to honor both the yin and the yang will, recognizing the value of the dance between intention and infinity. It is necessary to always honor your basic sense of abundance. This will develop your intuitive sense of timing, so that you will know when to sacrifice your body, when to stay up all night with your friend in the hospital, or when you plug away at your business plan until dawn. Likewise, you will know when to lie around and watch television

or take a long walk by the water. Instead of feeling burned-out or guilty, you will feel "right" with yourself, enlivened by your integrity, and wondrous at how real magic and synergy work.

One of the classic illustrations of this sense of the strength that results from balancing opposite forces is the caduceus, the Greek symbol of two snakes intertwined around a staff. Here, contraries—left and right, male and female, logical and emotional, life and death, night and day, waking and dreaming, meditation and action, above and below—are balanced and in dynamic harmony. This is an active alignment and not a stasis where nothing happens (a misaligned yin will) or a constant clash and war of opposites (a misaligned yang will). Empowered alignment is achieved through the creative interaction of the yin will with the yang will. When this occurs, manifestation involves no further effort: you find yourself in the right place at the right time with the right skills and preparation.

Do you have a developed sense of yang will or yin will in your life? Where are your forces of courage, clarity, and assertion, and where do you feel deep resources of energy? Is either of these currently undeveloped or in need of more attention? How can you bring these forces into alignment to better serve your work in the world?

THE PARADOX OF INTENTION

The paradox of intention involves learning how to want something while at the same time releasing your attachment to a specific result. This involves honoring your secondary processes by embracing ambiguity and uncertainty. Any vision or desire that you have received is asking to be honored. Shamanic teachings tell us that a vision not attended to can lead to illness. Such visions need not be grandiose; indeed they may often appear as challenges that need to be accepted fully. The process of manifestation, in this regard, often involves taking your pain and learning to transform it into art. I am speaking of art in its larger sense of putting everything in its right place. To open to the right place at the right time is to have space for everything and everyone. Your natural abundance allows you to open to any situation, to seeming confusion and dissonance, knowing that they too are creative forces asking for illumined expression.

The paradox of intention involves caring and not caring at the same time. This position of neutrality is the ideal place of manifestation, but it is not to be confused with detachment. Rather, it is a state of mind where you remain open to the full paradox of the caduceus, the two winding serpents. On the one hand, you really care, you want to do it well, and you want to make it happen. On the other hand, you completely let it go—you do not care at all and accept whatever happens openheartedly. Manifestation happens most effectively when you let go of grasping for specific results, but continue to move toward your goal, while continually adapting to new circumstances.

❧

Everyone begins a practice of abundance with certain intentions—they want to better themselves, to increase their material comfort, to reach beyond their current circumstances. But can you open to exploring how your intentions may actually be getting in the way of your deepest desires? When you look closely at your intentions, they are often symbolic of deeper needs. Perhaps you think you want a better job, but is that what you really want? Is it perhaps that you really want work that is meaningful to you? If so, your ultimate happiness is not dependent on finding a different job—and sometimes the incessant search for "the right job" can get in the way of your deepest desire, whose fulfillment may rely more on a reinterpretation and recommitment to your present work, transforming it into a source of deep satisfaction. Go back to your original list of what abundance and well-being mean to you. Examine each of the items on your list to see if you can determine what profound desire underlies each of your external desires. Can you find ways of bringing those deeper desires into your life right now, or of satisfying them directly, or of realizing how they are available to you in many ways in your present circumstances?

PRIMARY AND SECONDARY PROCESSES

Another of the contraries that the practice of conscious manifestation can bring into harmony is the dynamism of primary and secondary processes. A primary process is what you are consciously trying to accomplish, and it is usually aligned with the yang will—I am going to apply for this job; I am going to call someone who can help me market this idea. A secondary process is more associated with the yin will, and it is what happens to you while you are making other plans. You apply for one job and end up taking another—and perhaps better—job with the same company. You call someone for marketing advice and find out about a grant that will help fund another project. In other words, you are consciously trying to accomplish one thing but, if you keep your eyes and ears open, something else appears that may actually be better than what you had in mind.

Western cultures have been heavily weighted toward the yang will and primary processes. Success therefore is usually seen as the result of good planning, hard work, and follow-through. Stories of accidental discoveries—including Columbus's "discovery" of America, the discovery of penicillin, and the creation of Post-It notes—are often discounted as unreliable. But the importance of these secondary processes are very much a part of the Alchemy of Abundance, and part of the art of manifestation is to become aware of, to honor, and to consciously be open to the information from both the primary and secondary processes. A balanced dynamism between these two modalities will lead you toward more and more satisfying results, even if they are not what you originally intended. Honor the secondary processes, the unexpected—what you did not bargain for. This is often where the greatest richness in the path of manifestation lies.

〽

Can you identify the primary and secondary forces in your life that have been most important to you? Are there times when you have found greater benefit in these secondary processes than in your primary process? How can you open "closed narratives" in your life by paying attention to areas that you may have habitually ignored?

THE FOUR QUALITIES OF ATTENTION

Manifestation is not simply a matter of what we create or what visibly manifests, but also includes how we relate to what is happening, how we interpret what is going on, and how this fits into our sense of self. In this way, our attention is neither completely passive nor completely active, and it neither exists solely inside nor outside of oneself. Rather, it results from the ever-interweaving of our consciousness and our environment.

The basic "law of attention" says that wherever your attention is focused, your life will follow. Developing the ability to focus your attention is therefore crucial to the art and science of manifestation. How you receive and respond to the waves of information that greet you at every moment will determine what becomes visible in your life. Try this experiment. Walk down a city street or though a shopping mall when you are hungry. You will see and smell everything that is designed to appeal to the desire for food with an incredible intensity—a sign, a smell, a photograph of food will almost leap out at you, while everything else recedes. Then walk down the same street or mall when you are feeling sexy and see what your experience is like—you will see certain people as they pass, certain photographs, and certain window displays and not others. Although it is exactly the same street or shopping mall, your experience of it will be completely different, and everything you experience will take on new meanings and significance determined by your particular state of mind. Objectively, nothing has changed, but everything has changed in its significance.

One can observe at least four different qualities of attention, or ways in which we react to things that come into our awareness. The first is what Arnold Mindell has called "flirting." This quality is usually experienced as such a slight tickling of your awareness that your attention barely notices it. The second level is when something attracts your attention enough that you do become aware of it, but it does not move you into action in any way. You may still move right past it without being arrested by it, except perhaps on a subconscious level. The third level is when things demand your attention—when, whether you want to or not, you cannot brush them aside, like when you become aware of a rattle in your car engine. You hear it, you might not know what it is, but you know it is important. You know you will have to do something about it soon, but you can also schedule an appointment to take care of it. The fourth level is when something commands your attention: your car breaks down, you have a major illness, you get a phone call that your father has died, there is an earthquake, or you fall in love. In these moments you cannot schedule your dealing with the issue at your convenience; for often, at that moment, there is nothing else that is of any importance to you. Once you have understood the power of these four levels of attention to determine your experience, you will be able to work with them deliberately in your process of manifestation.

If your attention is too determined by unconscious forces or desires, you are likely to miss the most appropriate information for your current situation. The best way of working with your attention, then, is to keep your sensitivity wide open so that you can notice the great play of creation that goes on around you every day. In this way, you become aware not only of what you want to manifest, but also of what is calling out to you to come into being, and how to respond to the synchronicity of the moment.

Some people, who are addicted to the idea of doing great things may often be motivated by a lack of conscious attention. They are not aware of the abundance that is present in every moment, and they feel a need to create artificial melodramas or to begin great projects to overcome a felt lack of appreciation. In fact, most of us already have more than enough material around us already—we have closets stuffed with old photos, files full of data, and incomplete works to last a couple of lifetimes. So the practice of manifestation asks us to focus on the fulcrum of attention itself—how to work with it and develop it so that we do not create out of a sense of lack, but rather out of an ability to express our appreciation for what already exists. In this way, working with attention is part of the spiritual practice of daily life.

How do the four qualities of attention tend to operate in your life? Can you use this information to direct or redirect your attention? See if you can perform an experiment of actually changing your day solely through manipulating your attention. If you find that you are irritable and short-tempered, try to redirect your attention to what you are avoiding or missing that would actually bring you comfort and joy instead. If you can master this one skill, you will find that you will become an active creator of your experience and will be better able to focus on what is most important to you.

PLACE MAKING

One essential and often overlooked aspect of manifestation is growing roots; developing a literal sense of connectedness with a place. A primary characteristic of the absence of such rootedness is restlessness, a constant need to keep roaming through various careers, people, and other so-called opportunities with little sense of satisfaction. And while such frenzied mobility may be romanticized as a search to "find yourself," a nagging question arises: how can you be in so many places at once when you are nowhere at all?

Our home is our most basic manifestation of rootedness and it is a real place—a place where you can lie down, relax, and step out of the madness of incessant movement. At home, you can collect yourself and return to essence, and it is this return to your essence that allows you to experience the overflow of abundance that is the quintessence of the magical elixir of the alchemy of creativity.

Having a "deep sense of home," however, means a lot more than a literal dwelling place. "Home" is ultimately an unchallenged sense of belonging, and as this deepened experience of "home" expands out through your place in the world, it develops its own magic, its own vibrational field that surrounds you at all times.

Once, while on Pete Seeger's Clearwater sloop, which travels the Hudson River in upstate New York promoting environmental causes, we were told that the river was 450 million years old. When I returned home, I began looking for the river's earlier name. I searched through tourist Web sites, Hudson Valley guidebooks, and volumes on the Hudson River, but it was very difficult to find what this river had been called before it was named "Hudson." It almost seemed like a conspiracy of forgetfulness. Finally I found out that the Hudson was previously known as the Muhheakantuck, which means "The River That Flows Both Ways," referring to what we now call a tidal estuary, in which the waters from the sea flow upstream, while the fresh water flows downstream. (I am happy to say that this name is now prominently displayed on a New York State Department of Environmental Conservation sign at Waryas park by the river in Poughkeepsie, where I live.) Note how this earlier name derived from a visceral sense of place, not from someone who is said to have "discovered" it.

One of the most important achievements in manifestation work is reestablishing a visceral and intimate relationship with the land upon which we live—with the mountains, rivers, and particularities of the landscape. We can build temples to our landscape with our attention, and to honor them in this way is to experience their sacredness. We can return to these natural elements on a regular basis, clean up the trash, bring our family and children regularly to the rivers and the mountains of our natural environment, and make them a central pillar in our lives.

What kind of strength can be achieved by a deepened sense of belonging to a place? I have observed many times that when a person finds the right locale, the right living situation will often follow. For "timing" can never be separated from "spacing." When you are in the right place, the right time tends to manifest. One then gets to be part of a process that I call "Place Making." Place Making has to do with the interweaving of one's own story with the places where they have occurred. This relationship between a place and a story can root an entire community. It is common practice in the Apache tradition to have a story attached to every rock, tree, and mountain—so why not in Greenwich Village as well? "Here is the pump that didn't work because the vandals took the handles," and thus places become imprinted with the stories of their people.

An awareness of place also takes you down and inward, through the past and toward an integral sense of origin that lies below linear history and current condition. Among the earth-based aboriginal traditions of Australia, such awareness takes you inward into the realm of "the dreaming," where dreaming connects you to the larger mytho-poetic creation of the ancestors who now exist as part of the landscape.

Anyone who has ever been attached to a place knows how it can seep into one's bones, how it intertwines with all of one's motor and perceptual faculties. The smell of the earth gets into one's skin, the water gives the tea its unique flavor, and the colors and textures of the landscape become the fabric of one's interior landscape. To know the trees, the shrubs, the curvatures of the land, to till one's own soil, to eat food grown from the ground where you live and walk all becomes part of the manifestation process of Place Making.

There are a number of ways in which one's relationship to place can manifest. I know people who turn their homes into havens of generosity, hosting people from all over the world, becoming crucibles of understanding and bridges across cultures and generations as they create a new definition of family—an extended family that welcomes strangers as warmly as lifelong friends and relatives. Maintaining a sense of community like this creates a deepened and broader sense of home and expands our experience and understanding of environment.

How much do you know about the history of the place where you live? Do you know who lived on the land before the arrival your people? Take an interest in your landscape—see how much you can discover about your natural surroundings. Walk through your neighborhood and examine it as you would if you had traveled thousands of miles to visit a foreign country. Fill your journal with as much information as you can about the many facets of your natural environment.

RECONNECTING TO THE ENERGY OF SUBSTANCES

One extension of Place Making is a reconnection with the energy of substances. Just as every place has an essential nature that we can learn to experience directly, every substance we connect with—a chair, a table, a bell, or a pair of shoes—has an essence that is interacting with us. To rediscover the spirit within the things of our lives is to bring new soul-force into our experience.

When we begin to open to the consciousness of what is around us, the things of our lives cease to be mere objects. We can actually experience the life force within a tomato or the energy of an herbal infusion, as our experience of spirituality becomes deeply woven and enmeshed in the stuff and activities of our everyday life. By cultivating our attention in this way, we tap into a sense of sacredness that surrounds us and reflects our deep connection to everything and everyone. This cultivation process is the true "weaving" of the Tantra—the opening into the immanent awareness continuum that is ever-present and ever-sustaining. At this point, abundance ceases to be a concept, for it walks alongside you at every moment.

As you go through your day, try to connect with as many of the objects in your life as possible. Which have a lot of power for you? Which do you hardly notice? Do any of them have special meaning for you, or are there any that no longer have any meaning for you at all? Close your eyes and see how much of your living environment you can reconstruct in your imagination. Then open your eyes and see what you have missed. Are there objects in your environment with which you can find the kind of energy that will help you to see them and your life in new and more powerful ways?

REALIZING THE DIFFERENCE BETWEEN
OUR ROLES AND VOCATIONS

One evening, I turned to my then seven-year-old son and said, "It's nine o'clock. It's time to go to bed." As I said this, watching myself playing the role of father, I was laughing inside—listen to me! Here's a guy who's done whatever he's wanted to do all his life telling his kid that it's time to go to bed, and yet that was the role I was given in that moment to play. Understanding the importance of the roles you are asked to play in life is not necessarily about finding the right slot or even creating your own slot, but about learning how to become conscious of the relationship between your vocation and the roles you are asked to play in your life.

Some roles accrue to us naturally and effortlessly. Some people feel naturally at home in the arts, some people find themselves drawn to teaching, some people are natural parents, others feel most at home within an organization. In this way, an important part of the art of manifestation is to learn how to skillfully integrate ourselves with the roles that we have been given by central casting. As a colleague of mine once said about spirituality, you can play any spiritual game you want, but no matter what particular game you play, you need to play by the rules of that game. The main skill in this step of the Alchemy of Abundance is to learn to be clear about your place and function in this life, without getting caught in it. You need to come to a precise understanding of what you do in terms of who you are.

Defining your role is particularly important when you desire to create a professional practice in the world, whether it is a counseling practice, a law practice, a consulting practice, or anything else where working with others is involved. I call this practice "positive labeling." You cannot just announce yourself to the world and expect to be a success. First you must define and develop your particular service, project, or product. This gives potential customers a cognitive assurance that what you have to offer is valuable and workable. If your interaction with others is on the level of "Well, I work with energy medicine. I do a little healing, I do a little counseling," you are probably not going to get very far in the professional realm. People want to know specifically what they can expect from your services. Among business professionals, this is known as "branding."

Spend time defining specifically what it is that you have to offer. Create a label that communicates the essence of your service in a few words. This should be a label that represents the value of your work but also communicates it succinctly, a label that honors the essence of your work but is also one that others can understand. It is better, for example, to say that you are a Gestalt therapist or an astrological counselor or a marriage and family practitioner than to just say that you are a "counselor."

The following manifestation exercise can help you to define your role in life at this moment. It can also help you realize when your role no longer fits in with your current situation. Stand in front of a mirror and declare your current role in the form of a simple declarative statement: "I am a teacher." Or, "I am an airline pilot," "I am a corporate executive," "I am a peace officer." Feel the power of declaring your role/self-identity. Does it fit? Do you need to change it until it feels right, or abandon it altogether? If the naming of your current profession does not ring true, begin the sentence "I am," and wait for a response that feels genuine to you. You understand, of course, that your role is not your essence. Who you actually are lies far beyond societal ego-constructions. But you want to be able to feel your essence manifesting through your role. Sometimes, as you practice this, you will find yourself tweaking the statement to bring your essence in line with your role, "I am the cosmic shoe salesman who helps to ground all beings," for example. As you practice this, you begin to feel better about your work because you are aligning it with your vibrational essence. Eventually, as you build power and clarity, you start saying it aloud to other people as well as to the mirror. "I'm a poet," "I'm an artist," or "I'm a cook." Being able to "declare" your role, your mission, is at least half of the battle.

Once you feel more aligned with your current role in life, you want to know that you can be successful at it. "Do I have the proper qualifications?" "Will I be able to feed my family and pay my mortgage with this?" These are important and legitimate questions, but I want to emphasize that they are secondary to the power of your conviction, which is built through your declaration. Say it to yourself, and announce your calling to your friends. A colleague of mine said that the first day he was able to get up and announce that he was healer was the moment that his lifework opened up and blossomed.

When you consciously take on a role, you realize that it is not just your individual whim, but it is, in essence, the way you are intended to support civilization. This is where abundance makes its connection with greatness and where it connects with the concept of one's *dharma*. In Sanskrit the word dharma refers not only to your role in life, or your station, or your vocation, but it also means literally that which sustains your existence. Embracing your role in life is what inspires a captain to go down with his ship. To sacrifice yourself for others while embodying your role is to fully embrace your place in life—"I am captain of this ship. I will go down with this ship." I am not speaking of martyrdom or a misaligned sense of duty here. Rather, I am speaking of how a true sense of responsibility for your place; your "station," whatever and wherever it may be, becomes part of the conscious practice of manifestation. It is the responsibility of a parent setting healthy limits for young children, the assurance—communicated to others—that you will show up on time and do your job. Such action develops consistency, which develops power, the power of virtue. You begin with the acknowledgment of who and what you are, in terms of your role, and move toward sustaining and supporting the world with your work.

The deeper you move into conscious manifestation, the more the importance of this law is revealed to you. When you take note of everything that happens while you are performing your role in life, you will often notice that karmic reactions occur very quickly, almost instantaneously, because you have begun to develop an intense clarity about the correlations between your thoughts, moods, reactions, and external events.

❧

Make a list of the roles in your life. Make this list as long and detailed as possible. See if you can identify the number of roles you play in a single day. For instance, when the phone rings, consider for a moment the many roles that you may be asked to play—will you become the parent, the child, the friend, the lover, or the co-worker? Do the exercises included in this chapter about investigating what your role is in your current life. What is your primary role? How comfortable are you in that role? What roles would you like to play, what roles do you feel you are being called to play, which roles are no longer satisfying to you? Talk to your friends and associates about your deepest dreams. See if you can speak in the first person declarative: i.e., "I am a photographer—I am at my best when I am capturing images on film that reveal the true nature and significance of what I see."

HONORING YOUR AGREEMENTS

When you honor your agreements with other people, you are taking both your own values and your responsibility to others seriously. When you honor your agreements you are also creating strong karmic bonds with others that will nourish you and those around you.

An important part of successful manifestation in this regard is to use negotiation processes as a means to clarify your agreements with others. An aligned negotiation process is not simply a means to get what you want, but is a way to establish clarity and mutual agreement. Such a process rarely succeeds through easy formulas and can more often than not be a long ongoing pilgrimage. But pilgrimage empowers the soul and forges connections that endure, while formulas do not.

A while back, I heard an elderly Tibetan monk speak about the inhuman tortures he had endured for over thirty years in Chinese prisons. Someone in the audience asked how he had been able to endure such treatment for so long. The monk explained that when a fellow monk was dying and asking for water, he had offered him spittle from his own mouth. The dying monk had pulled him close and told him that he must make it through this ordeal to go out and tell the world what had happened. And the monk drew power from this agreement; it strengthened his will and gave him the courage to live. On his own, he might have succumbed, but the power of commitment to another gave him renewed determination and life.

A number of years ago, the college where I teach was in contact with a potential donor who wanted to endow a considerable sum of money for "Jungian Studies." A number of people in the administration were suspicious of "Jungian Studies," thinking it to be uncritical and cultish, and the development office was ready to scrap the project. Some of us, however, saw this as a tremendous opportunity to move higher education into new directions. We brought representatives of the two parties together and talked for over a year, during which we kept shifting the language, reformulating intentions, and building a consensus of purpose. In the end, the college received a large endowment for "embodied learning and the mythic imagination." The money and energy from this endowment has brought incredible teachers and teachings into the college: mindfulness training, movement awareness, embodied physics, contemplation, and the American landscape, all because people had the patience and openness to stay with the process of negotiation.

Do you keep your agreements? See if you can catch yourself when you blame others, make excuses, or explain situations away when you are unable to honor your agreements. When you make an agreement make it as conscious a process as possible. Do not see it as a tentative agreement, as something that you can explain away later if you are unable to follow through with it. Engage fully in the negotiation process so that everyone understands exactly what is being asked of him or her and what he or she can expect. See each agreement, no matter how small, as something of immense importance to you, and then develop a process by which you mindfully and respectfully deal with situations in which you become aware that you are going to be unable to meet your agreements. Can you go to the other person and discuss the situation as soon as possible, not waiting until the deadline has come and gone before informing them?

THE IMPORTANCE OF LOVE

Many people when they hear the word love think only of romantic love. But in terms of the Alchemy of Abundance, love takes on a myriad of forms. When we are following our genuine path, there is a quality of love to whatever we do: there is the love of the carpenter for the wood, the sailor for the sea, the artist for the texture of the paint, the counselor for the consulting room. In this sense, whatever we are working with becomes our altar as the various fragrances of sacredness permeate our lives. The loss of this scent of sacredness obscures the variegated and blissful manifestation of divinity, which is perhaps why so much has been made in the West of the concept of romantic love, where these divinities still speak to us is through our romantic or sexual connections.

When we are walking on our own path, we release a lot of pressure that often comes with placing so much importance on any one area of our lives—or on any one particular outcome. In the Alchemy of Abundance, we allow our love for life to manifest its fullness in all of its variant possibilities. When we walk in openness and acceptance, we discover that no matter what our circumstances, we are walking in a world of overflowing abundance. We are less concerned with the desire to dominate, influence, or impress anybody, or with being seen as a success, and thus have more room in our lives for genuine interactions and connections.

Can you list all of the various forms of love that exist in your life right now? After each item on your list, see if you can uncover the deeper significance of each of these kinds of love in your life. Can you see how it is a deep desire *to* love—not necessarily to *be* loved—that motivates many of the most satisfying experiences in your life?

CHAPTER
THREE

Challenges to the Alchemy of Abundance

TIME

The first challenge to the Alchemy of Abundance is time. In many ways, this is not only a personal issue, but a cultural one as well. We all know we need to slow down, but how can we when we feel that there is never enough time to get things accomplished? Are there alternatives to rushing through your day with feelings of resentment and dissatisfaction?

Through the practice of the Alchemy of Abundance, we can come to understand that we have all the time in the world. When we release our anxieties around specific outcomes or not getting everything accomplished, the entire field in front of us transforms. This issue was seen in alchemical traditions as relating to the Moon, which represented reconnection to the inherent cycles of one's life. Monday is the Moon's day. Although I know this is unrealistic for most people, I have not worked on Monday in years. I make it a part of my practice to leave Mondays for lunar concerns: open-breathed relaxation, writing down my dreams, and becoming aware of the natural flow between my inner and outer worlds. But if you cannot or do not want to go that far, you can leave a space at the end of each day for reflection, a space where you honor the importance of slowing down and opening up to experience the flow of events in your daily life as part of the great tapestry of creation.

Gnostics and others said that the first test one was given after death, the test of time, was related to the Moon. The idea being that, if you could open to the deep soul-memory (also ruled by the Moon) of who you are, an incarnation would be nothing more than another day in the life of the soul. You could relax because you would actually have perceived that you have all the time you will ever need to do and experience whatever you need to experience.

※

How do you spend your day? Do you spend your time doing the things you love, the things that bring you a sense of satisfaction? Can you imagine arranging your life in some way that makes room for those things that are most important to you? If you have ever experienced a serious medical situation involving yourself or others, you may have discovered that the responsibilities of your usual life somehow seemed to take care of themselves, whereas the most important things in your life—talking with friends, spending time in quiet contemplation, reaching out to others, performing work that brings you a deep sense of satisfaction—are often the things that you had not made a high-enough priority. Can you begin, therefore, to recreate your life in ways that make the best use of your time; ways that feed your creativity and your sense of the natural abundance available to you in every moment?

THE ALIGNED USE OF WILL AND POWER

Another challenge in the Alchemy of Abundance is the right and aligned use of will and power. In the alchemical tradition, this refers to your willingness to hold the sword of the warrior, and to take that sword in your hand knowing that the sword contains both power and danger. If your power is misaligned, you become a workaholic or you get thoughtless speeding tickets or engage in inappropriate anger or begin to lead a lifestyle of constant irritation. But the other side of the sword—its sharpness—relates to your gifts, your power, and your abilities to transform the world, to do well, to make things happen. The tip of the blade of the sword is your intention, and having a clear and focused intention is one consequence of the right use of will. Some people block this energy by refusing to engage it, by trying to opt out of power altogether, but that is like trying not to breathe. What we want to do in the practice of manifestation is to work with the tensions of wanting, to see these tensions as inherent aspects of the conscious cultivation of an awakened will. In this way we learn to sort out what is vital and important from what is not, and cut through the field of distraction that most people experience as daily life.

The conscious cultivation of attention is much like working with a yoga posture. In yoga, you go into a posture and that takes effort, power, and will. But if you just stay fixed in that position, you do not become flexible. To make progress in yoga, you have to learn how to breathe into that posture. You experience the tension, and you gradually open your flexibility by cultivating the contraries of tension and release. It is this balance of strength and flexibility that we aim for in the Alchemy of Abundance. This balance involves the skillful interplay of tension, intention, and attention. It is not that stress is bad; stress has its uses. Stress can save your life if you are in a critical situation, but to be overwhelmed by stress is to lose the power inherent in the healthy balance of strength and flexibility. The skillful interplay of tension and release, intention and attention is both our method and our goal.

Many of your accomplishments in life have resulted from the applied use of your power and will. These two aspects of the yang will are very important when they are working in alignment with your life force and current priorities. In what ways can you further bring your power and will into alignment with your deepest wishes?

AMBIGUITY, MULTIPLICITY, AND SUBTLETY

Another challenge we face on this journey is that of opening to ambiguity, multiplicity, and subtlety. Certainty is the enemy of conscious manifestation when it leads to rigidity, attachment, and skewed data—not that you lie outright, but when you are "certain," there is a tendency to ignore or embellish anything that does not fit in with your idea of how things should be. In the Alchemy of Abundance, it is not a question of what you believe or do not believe, but rather of being open to the Tantra, the woven texture of the way things are.

If you open to ambiguity, how do you know if you should stay or if you should go? How can you tell if you are in the right place? Staying tuned to the energetic quality of your vision is one way through this difficult place. This is an important part of the process because very often the group with whom you are associating will influence your vision and perception. But if you are in direct contact with your own quality of purpose, you can sense a situation in which the collective is no longer resonating with your values.

When you feel you are in a place where you do not belong, the habitual response is to complain and make everybody else miserable around you. The Alchemy of Abundance puts the responsibility squarely on your shoulders. First you should ask, what am I learning from this situation? Is there something in me that needs to change? Sometimes this means that you should find someone with whom you can talk about your situation. When you discuss the situation, you should try as much as possible to relate the details as clearly and objectively as possible—try as hard as you can not to mislead or misconstrue the facts in order to get sympathy and support.

All that may be necessary to find your proper place in the world is finding others who can validate your vision. You need to be seen in a new way. You need to find others who are interested in your ideas, your service, or the products of your vision. Sometimes you just need a pat on the back. Being motivated to seek out others for insight and assurance is one of the most important steps in the Alchemy of Abundance. Since manifestation cannot occur in a vacuum, you want to keep your antennae out for traditions, lineages, and places where you feel a sense of belonging.

Sometimes when you begin to suffer, you realize that it is because you no longer fit into a particular slot. The quality of feeling is your barometer, and it can reveal true direction. A colleague of mine sold cosmetics for a living, which she actually liked to do, but she could no longer in good conscience participate in an environment where sales were done by quotas. What she enjoyed was the personal contact, the practice of helping clients and making them happy. She was torn between the parts of her job that she loved and those that were downright distasteful. She spent weeks wondering if she should stay or leave until one day she heard her heart say very clearly that her job was going to kill her. Although the messages we receive are not always so clear, if we are willing to examine the true nature of our feelings and how they align with our current situations, what to do becomes obvious. And when this realization comes to you, the power of abundance moves you to stop hurting yourself, to release worrying about how others will react, to move out, or in, to take your place.

In almost every situation there comes a moment when you have to ask yourself, "Should I stay or should I go?" Make a list of any current commitments where you may have a question of this nature. Then list all of the positive and negative aspects of staying and leaving. What would it be possible for you to learn if you stayed? What possibilities does staying in your current situation prevent you from exploring? Ask yourself if you have given 100 percent the situation. Allow yourself to visualize the scenario around your staying or leaving: which one has more juice, more power, more lifeforce? Where are you ready to take action?

DISAPPOINTMENT

Another major challenge is learning how to deal with deep disappointment. You may one day have to face the fact that you will not write the great American novel or run the hundred-yard dash in record time. This is the crucial moment when you wake up to the disillusionment—when you see your dream before you dissolving.

If you can hold this energy and breathe it in fully, instead of pushing it away, what will happen is it will literally burn up inside of you, but it will not destroy you. You will still have everything you have always had inside, but there will be a reckoning—an awakening to limitation. This moment can result in a great epiphany that frees and empowers you. It took a great amount of energy to believe in the possibility of something that was never going to happen, and now, instead of being in a constant state of struggle and stress and regret and disappointment, you will be free to discover where your path is leading you.

So whatever the disappointment is—not getting a promotion, losing a relationship, getting your book rejected, your business falling apart, not being as healthy as you may like to be—this is a place where you can work with it in a deep and radical way by not pushing it away or denying it, but breathing it in, being with that disappointment, letting that disappointment burn through you, feeling its fullness. It is best to allow disappointment and challenges and their concomitant emotions to course through you and transform themselves rather than holding on to regrets and resentments that will only complicate things in the future.

Our deepest lines of purpose are reawakened through just such adversity. During these periods, you will often go through a period of rudderlessness, of confusion, of not knowing what to do. One workshop participant put it this way. "People say that when one door closes, another door opens, but there can be a long hallway in between them and I am in that hallway." The practice of abundance says that when you are in that hallway, let yourself be in the hallway, let yourself get to the bottom of the confusion, let yourself be with whatever process is going on. These periods of transition need to be embraced with openness, compassion, and, above all, patience. The practice of abundance gives you the faith to take the road that has not been taken, to go through the dark wood instead of trying to force a change that is not ready to happen. Remember that if you can stay open, the greater the crisis, the greater the reward.

One of my great models of working with ideals in this regard comes from Ralph Waldo Emerson, who said when his six-year-old son died, "I am defeated every day, but to victory, I am born." Are you born to victory? Of course you are. To abandon your ideals because of disappointment is a form of depression. When you work with the Alchemy of Abundance, you need to remember that human evolution is infinitesimally slow. It was not long ago that women could not vote; not many years ago before that there was slavery in the United States. It is important to remember that even if you have not been able to change the world immediately, that does not mean that your ideals have failed. Rather, the process of conscious manifestation is to remain connected with your ideals, to allow your life to be fueled by your authentic ideals, and not to lose hope in the future possibilities that you hold in your heart.

Make a list of the major disappointments in your life—things you would have liked to have happened, but did not; accomplishments you would have liked to have achieved that you did not, relationships that ended despite your wishes. Following each of these entries, see if you can list all of the good things that entered life only because these desires were frustrated. The end of one relationship sometimes allows you to create a new and better one. To miss out on one job opportunity will often make it possible for you to take a more personally satisfying one.

CHAPTER
FOUR

Creating a Lifestyle of Abundance

THE LIFESTYLE of Scott and Helen Nearing is an elegant example of the possibility of organizing your daily life in a way that feeds your creativity and abundance. In *Living the Good Life*, the Nearings wrote about their experience of moving out of the city and into the country and learning to grow their own food, trying, in Thoreau's words, "to live deliberately." The Nearings' goal was to create a lifestyle in which four hours of each day were dedicated to working for sustenance, four hours for creative pursuits, and four hours for socializing with friends. Even with these twelve hours taken, they still had another twelve hours to sleep and eat and to do whatever else they wanted or needed to do. They were able to accomplish this by living on very little money, with a lot of spirit. How many of us in our complex and materially sophisticated society can even approach the Nearing's goal of "four," "four," and "four"? But since one must begin at the beginning, I want to offer some concrete practices that can lead you to more elegance, clarity, and consciousness.

FROM REFLECTION TO PRACTICE

First, find something you can do on a regular basis that puts you in connection with your own creativity and natural sense of abundance, whether it is painting, walking in the park, swimming, or watering your plants. If you can develop a regular practice that puts you in the flow of life, that practice will begin to draw in the circumstances that will move your life toward the rhythm of natural abundance, rather than moving to someone else's agenda.

Another everyday Alchemy of Abundance practice is to take deep breaths while waiting for red lights. Our energy tends to rush around traffic stops: "I'm in a hurry! Can't they go faster? What's wrong with them?" Such indulgence will not only raise your blood pressure, it will condition you to impatience and scarcity—to the experience of never having enough time. So, in these types of moments, you can slow down and breathe deeply and deliberately. Then, instead of the usual experience of rushing everywhere and never actually arriving anywhere because you are always thinking of where you have to rush to next, you begin to notice everything that you have been missing. Maybe it is the beauty of the autumn leaves, or the smiles on people's faces in the park, or the sound of laughter in the car next to yours. At times, in quiet moments of complete attention, the experience of waiting for a light to turn green can become a timeless moment of beauty. You are almost apprehensive at being so full of bliss, that when the light turns green, you will have lost all desire to drive anywhere. It is in this way that you can begin to understand just how much of life you are missing when you are rushing from place to place, and how complete satisfaction is available to us in every moment—no matter how mundane—once you understand that the quality of your experience is completely under your control. The consciousness that you opened to, in moments like these, will carry over to other moments of your life as well.

Another powerful practice of abundance that you can consciously incorporate into your daily life is the "vacuum cleaner meditation." Before going to sleep, take a moment to stop and round up everything that you have been thinking about—your unfinished business, your plans for tomorrow, something you left on your desk, or whatever—and just imagine that you have a psychic vacuum cleaner that can pull in everything and let it disappear. Being preoccupied with what we think we have to do or remember prevents us from receiving new and powerful possibilities. This clearing exercise can leave you open enough to receive new ideas and information. Your days will have a sense of completion. Time will open; there will be fresh perspectives, and you will be able to see more clearly what you really desire. Every morning and night allow yourself to touch your own divinity—be open enough to hear the still small voice inside of you. As a derivative of this practice, your sleeping process will invariably become one of relaxation and release where you can receive whatever insights and messages through your dream and "in-between" states.

Another practice of abundance is to go for one hour each day without complaining. This can actually take some effort, but if you can do it for an hour, then try it for half a day, and then try not to complain for a day or even a week. This does not mean that you give up caring about what is happening around you or how it affects you. It does not mean that you are not aware of what needs to be done or how it should be done—you remain fully engaged but simultaneously release the habit of complaining. In this way you begin to be actively supportive; you find that you have radically altered the way that you are interacting with others. This fresh interweaving with others will reveal a vast net surrounding you that supports you more, and in more ways than you ever imagined. As you incorporate these daily practices of abundance into your days, you will experience your life in a new way and realize the abundance that is woven into every moment of your life.

CHAPTER
FIVE

The Mandala of Manifestation

THE ALCHEMY OF ABUNDANCE involves interweaving the external with the internal, the circumstances of our life with our meditative imagination. If we only do the external practices of abundance, we may develop "new muscles" and be able to create circumstances that are to our liking, but we may not have the depth and insight that opens new vistas of consciousness. And if we only do meditative processes, we may open to new areas of perception and awareness, but we may not be able to integrate them into our day-to day life. Working with the "Mandala of Manifestation" allows you to weave a Tantric tapestry out of the meditative dimension and your day-to-day life. Through the exercises included in the Mandala of Manifestation, you create a "feedback loop" between your inner and outer worlds, with one enriching and deepening the other, as you build your own personal Temple of Beauty.

JOURNEYING TO THE MANDALA OF MANIFESTATION

Now that we have discussed the general principles and practices of the Alchemy of Abundance, it is time for you to investigate how this process is currently operating in your life. In the following exercises, you will create your own Mandala of Manifestation that will help you develop and deepen your own manifestation practice.

On the enclosed CD, I have included fourteen guided visualizations. Each of them explores a different facet of the Mandala of Manifestation by allowing you to examine specific areas in your life. In the first visualization, we journey to the great Temple of Manifestation itself. It is imagined as located in Delphi, Greece, where it was said to be the Omphalos, the center of the world. This temple is shaped like a giant circle, with an opening in the center that contains a central altar. Surrounding the altar are twelve separate chambers, each of which holds a particular aspect of life energy.

Most of the work you will be doing in this part of the program will be personal work—you will explore, through these twelve chambers, what has been attracting or demanding your attention, as well as what your optimum response would be. As you continue with this work, you are encouraged to return to these chambers to continually deepen your awareness of how to positively and power-fully engage these forces in your life.

After you have visited one of these chambers via the guided visualizations, it is important that you create your own Mandala of Manifestation, a visual representation of how these twelve aspects are operating in your life right now. You can start this process by setting up your mandala before beginning, and then filling it out with whatever you learn in each exploration. Take a large sheet of paper and draw a circle on it. Divide this large circle into twelve "slices." On the outside of this circle, write the words for each chamber, as listed below, in a clockwise direction, with number 10, "Vocation," at the top position and number 4, "Home," in the bottom position.

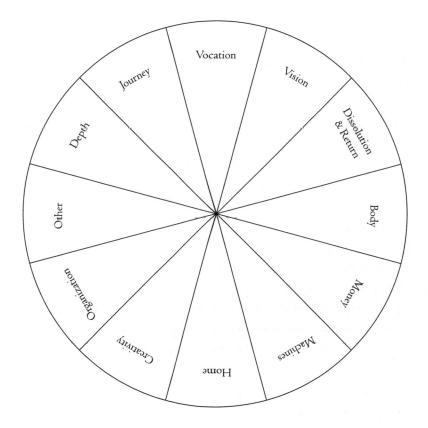

Then, after you finish each guided journey into these different chambers, use the spaces in this mandala to draw or write whatever you saw or experienced that moved you during the visualization. I also recommend that you use your journal to collect your thoughts and experiences while moving through these guided journeys into your Mandala of Manifestation. I find that the most effective journal for this kind of work is one that combines both written words and visual images—either ones that you draw yourself or collect elsewhere.

As you continue this program, if you discover other insights or new thoughts about each of these individual forces, return to your mandala and journal and incorporate them, so that your mandala develops along with your understanding. You can include meaningful quotations, poems, tarot or prayer cards, illustrations and photographs from magazines and newspapers, original drawings, or whatever powerfully resonates with the issues explored in each of these chambers. In this way, you will have an ongoing "mirror" that reflects the forces that are in play at this moment in your life. You may soon find that the images in your mandala begin to move into your dreams and interface with your waking reality.

The integration of these three aspects from your practice of the Alchemy of Abundance—the guided visualizations, the journal work, and the visual mandala (along with material from your waking reality and your dreams)—is perhaps the most important aspect of this program. By diligently working through this process, you will learn to weave the different threads of manifestation together. As the practice deepens, it will begin to reveal the secrets of your own personal path, letting you know where you need to focus your attention. Remember, it is the quality and focus of your attention that determines what manifests in your life.

These individual guided visualizations are designed to be experienced in the order in which they are presented, but if you feel you need to return to a particular chamber before completing the circle, you can return to any of them, as often you like. Once you have gone through the entire series, I recommend that you start the CD from the beginning and go through the whole cycle in one sitting, which will take eighty minutes. There are insights and correspondences between each of the chambers that will only become obvious when experienced in this way. But until you have completed the series of visualizations, it is important to experience each of these journeys on its own. Each of the exercises can be completed in less than eight minutes, but be sure to include plenty of time after completing the visualization to work on your mandala. Although much of what you will experience will be made clear though the visualization process itself, the work you will be doing to create your mandala is a most important part of this process.

As you return to these visualizations in the future, be sure to continue to work on your journal and to create new Mandalas of Manifestation representative of your current situation and understanding. Many people like to review, or at least refer to, their previous mandalas and journals to refresh their memory of aspects that were important to them in the past, and review how their creative process has changed and accelerated by using these exercises. For this reason, it is very important to date your mandalas. This will enable you to track the recurrence of certain forms and figures in each of the chambers as they continue to reveal themselves to you in stronger and more profound ways.

ENTERING THE TEMPLE OF BEAUTY

The Temple of Manifestation is also known as the "Temple of Beauty," "beauty" being one meaning of the word "cosmos"—the divine order that we are in the process of aligning with. As you enter this temple, you will investigate what has been happening in the last year of your life, who has been around you, what pathways you have been trying to develop, what situations you have been trying to let go of, what obstacles and challenges cling to you like barnacles that you

LISTEN TO TRACK 1
Entering the Temple of
Manifestation

cannot pull off. You will examine the quality of energy in this last year of your life and what the fabric of manifestation has looked like around you.

THE FIRST CHAMBER: BODY

The Mandala of Manifestation begins with your awareness of and relationship to your body. Once you have taken form, your first experience is "I am." In the Alchemy of Abundance, you begin by learning to honor your body, to listen to its messages, and to fall in love with your current embodiment. The desire to be and to become is born with your embodiment. To smother the flame of desire is to extinguish life itself. This flame is akin to the heat applied to the alembic, the vessel used in the practice of alchemy to eventually reveal the philosopher's stone.

During this and other meditations, it is important to be completely honest and nonjudgmental about your responses. There are no right answers, or answers that are better than others—the only important answers are your answers, because this is meant to be an investigation of your core thoughts and feelings. It is your true feelings about the issues revealed in the various chambers of the mandala that can empower the creation of new experience. Once you understand and accept your current feelings and beliefs, you can see what is necessary in order for you to proceed from exactly where you are to where you want to be. So one last process you can do before leaving the chamber is to envision its highest form of manifestation in your life.

LISTEN TO TRACK 2
Body

Everyone's path is going to be different, but the only path that has any value to you is your own, no matter how it evolves through time.

THE SECOND CHAMBER: MONEY

In the second chamber we move from "I am" to "I have." Here you look at all of the issues and circumstances you have surrounding money: your money, other people's money, as well as your possessions. Note the feelings and attitudes you hold toward your finances, as well as toward those things that are important to you. What financial styles do you feel most comfortable with? What would be your optimum manifestation in this realm? To get the most benefit from this, allow your creative imagination to take you beyond concepts into concrete images and powerful feelings. This is where manifestation can happen.

LISTEN TO TRACK 3
Money

THE THIRD CHAMBER: MACHINES

Machines have infiltrated our lives to a much larger degree than we ordinarily acknowledge. Not long ago, most everyone could perform basic repairs on their automobiles and the other common machines in their lives, but nowadays most people do not even know how their machines work. Ultimately, machines are nothing more than extensions of our creative power and manifestations of our desires. Their supposed dark side is a direct manifestation of our own chaos, experienced as the hectic pace of life, technical breakdowns, and lack of personal contact. This third chamber is where we look at the machines in our lives not as demons or saviors but as forms we can learn to work with in an appropriate manner. We investigate our relationship to all the devices in our lives as well as technology in general.

LISTEN TO TRACK 4
Machines

THE FOURTH CHAMBER: HOME

In this chamber you explore every aspect of your home—from its furnishings to its ambience—and even the neighborhood in which you dwell. Your home also includes every living being present in your home—your partners, relatives, children, pets, and even the spirits of the past. Allow your home to guide you through it as you discover what your home is saying to you. How at home are you in your home? What is the fullest vision of what you want your home to be?

LISTEN TO TRACK 5
Home

THE FIFTH CHAMBER: CREATIVITY

Once you have established your rootedness, you can expand into your creative power. With a solid foundation to your enterprise, you can take risks; you can open to new possibilities. Very often in our dreams, these new possibilities appear as children. In this way, the fifth chamber is the realm of both creativity and the child. Those of us who are parents know that childbirth itself is the greatest miracle of manifestation. Every birth, be it of a child or an idea, is a new incarnation of divine possibility. Allow yourself to open here to your widest purview of creative energy. What would this look like and feel like? What inner landscapes does it produce within you—landscapes that are seeking to be born into the world?

The divinely inspired creativity of the muse also appears in this realm. In some mysterious way, the muse appears—in a chance meeting or the words of a friend or the witnessing of a work of art—and suddenly music arises, or poetry appears. This is the realm in which we also discover playfulness as an essential aspect of manifestation, and the opening to its enthusiasm.

LISTEN TO TRACK 6
Creativity

THE SIXTH CHAMBER: ORGANIZATION

In the sixth chamber, the creative energy of the adolescent ego learns to offer itself in service to humanity. This chamber houses the process of distillation, understood as "I reason, I discriminate, and I place things in order." This area also relates to the process of digestion, in which the body makes a decision as to what is nurturing and what has to be let go. In the sixth chamber, you will observe your day-to-day routine—the ongoing organization of your life, including your daily schedule, how you interact with your immediate environment, and the habits and rituals you have around eating. Once you become aware of the energies that are attracting or demanding your attention here, allow yourself to envision the feeling quality of the ideal flow of an ideal day.

LISTEN TO TRACK 7
Organization

THE SEVENTH CHAMBER: OTHER

We often begin a program of manifestation seeking to have our desires fulfilled and our needs met. But in the seventh chamber we come to realize that we rarely know what our true needs and desires are. How many of us know ourselves so completely that we know exactly what is good for us at any given moment? What is actually good for us is often mysteriously connected to our relationships, because nobody can meet their own needs alone. This realm of relationship is in many ways the most powerful of all secondary processes. Here is where our individual plans often crumble in the face of what happens. In the chamber of relationship, our intention is revealed as only one piece of the complex process of manifestation. No matter what our intentions may be, we come to understand that our manifestation in the world is intimately connected with everyone else's manifestations. Hence, in the seventh chamber, we examine all of our significant relationships with friends, siblings, co-workers, partners, lovers, and associates. What messages have you been receiving through your meetings with others? What might they be asking of you?

LISTEN TO TRACK 8
Other

THE EIGHTH CHAMBER: DEPTH

The essence of the eighth chamber is the descent into whatever lurks below. The realm of death resides here, along with the underworld and its spirits, decomposition, and loss in its myriad forms. Another aspect of the eighth chamber is sexuality, including the erotic imagination, fantasy, seduction and power. Both of these realms—sexuality and death—stretch our ego beyond its personal limits and into the unknown. Both of these areas are also places where our shadows often reside—the disowned parts of ourselves and our lives; places of shame, scandal, and darkness: aspects of our lives that we would rather not see. This is where the "wrathful deities," as they are called in Tibetan Buddhism, appear before us—aggression, anger, greed, envy, and revenge, whatever it is that we keep below the surface.

The Alchemy of Abundance asks us to engage these energies fully and completely, so that we can arrive at their richness in the way that natural processes can turn coal into a diamond, or a speck of sand into a pearl. How has death or sexuality been attracting or demanding your attention? What messages are being given to you? Where are they asking you to go? Be fearless in your explorations, trusting that anything and everything that is brought to your attention contains a seed of healing and resolution.

LISTEN TO TRACK 9
Depth

THE NINTH CHAMBER: JOURNEY

The ninth chamber has to do with the awakening of faith—moments when you experience a sense of the divine or the presence of a cosmic intelligence in your life and moments when you feel, as the poet Walt Whitman said, "Now in a moment, I know what I am for." This is the chamber of spiritual quests, of awakening and reawakening to your sense of the true meaning of your life. The challenge in the ninth chamber is to learn how to be open and receptive to the continual reawakening of your relationship with the divine.

LISTEN TO TRACK 10
Journey

THE TENTH CHAMBER: VOCATION

The tenth chamber of the Mandala of Manifestation has to do with creating circumstances that will allow you to play your most effective role in the world, while ennobling your spirit, rather than destroying or compromising it within the marketplace. In the tenth chamber, vocation is seen as more than career or station. It is where we polish and maintain our spiritual values, including integrity, balance, and our sense of purpose, as we navigate through the marketplace. Imagine yourself in the working environment that most perfectly expresses your soul's energy and purpose. Where are you? Who are you with? What kind of activity is going on? Remember, if you can see it, you can be it.

LISTEN TO TRACK 11
Vocation

THE ELEVENTH CHAMBER: VISION

The eleventh chamber of the mandala is where vocation expands into vision. Great vision requires daring, and in order to have daring, you need to have ideals. The teachings of manifestation in this realm of our experience have to do with the conscious use of ideals that can keep you connected to a deep sense of hope in humanity and in our collective destiny. Misaligned ideals and idealism serve as smokescreens or excuses for our not participating fully in the world. But our ideals need not be abstract constructs that we are always trying to live up to. You do not have to reach your ideals, you simply need to allow your ideals to emerge from within you and let them inspire you to be greater, more open, and more free. Ideals always take you to the future, not as an escape from the present, but because they point you toward what you intuit is possible. Such ideals and visions are both the building blocks of our greater future, and the springboards through which we transcend the limits of time and space.

LISTEN TO TRACK 12
Vision

THE TWELFTH CHAMBER: DISSOLUTION AND RETURN

The twelfth and final chamber in the Mandala of Manifestation is that of dissolution. Here we return to the question of the unmade bed. If everything we shall ever do or experience will be forgotten, what will ultimately determine the quality of our lives? Is it the legacy we leave? Is it fame—Achilles choosing a short life of fame rather than a good life of anonymity? Or might it be consciousness itself—our awareness that shines on through the play of forms. When you go to bed each night, you dissolve back into the source to re-emerge in the morning. Breathing in and out, you dissolve and re-emerge at each moment; life and death flow as the passing of our days. But through this all, there is the quality of the deep heart, the potential through every breath, every day, every life, to awaken, to let go and re-emerge in deeper and more blissful communion with everything and everyone.

When you have completed your visit to the twelfth chamber of manifestation, allow the CD to play the final track, "Leaving the Temple of Manifestation." This will complete your introduction to the Temple of Beauty. Remember that you can return at any time, with the assistance of these guided visions or not, to revisit and revision any areas that are of concern to you.

LISTEN TO TRACK 13
Dissolution & Return

When you have gone through the cycle of visualizations in the Temple of Beauty, you will have a complete Mandala of Manifestation that you can keep working with for deeper explorations and attunement. Be sure to date your mandala so that you will be able to refer to it in the future, and think about hanging it up in a place where you will see it every day before you leave the house—by a bedroom mirror, on the kitchen refrigerator, or in your meditation room. You will soon be able to see the patterns in your mandala evolving and interacting in new and powerful ways and witness the awesome wisdom that connects every aspect of your life. You will be a tantric weaver, weaving the fabric of your destiny and existence, just as you are deeply woven into it, co-creating with the divine forces of the cosmos.

LISTEN TO TRACK 14
Leaving the Temple
of Manifestation

CHAPTER
SIX

Creating an Abundant Society

THE WEAVING PROCESS of manifestation encompasses the breadth of life, death, and beyond. But there is always return, a return to being grounded in this world. Wherever you may go, you will return to here, to what is and what has to be done. Spiritual pathways and commercial routes, therefore, cannot be separated. Indeed, they never have been. It was the merchants after all who brought the Buddha over the Silk Road to China, and the British East India Company opened the way for yoga to come to the west. Every monastery has someone who is responsible for the institution's endowment and for maintaining the political connections that ensure the safety and security of the order. Every one of us who pays taxes, balances a checkbook, or uses a credit card is obliged to be his or her own accountant on a daily basis before or after sitting in meditation. The spirituality of the future, therefore, will be one that is woven together with a work ethic that supports justice, sustainability, and abundance; integrating our personal processes with the social and economic structures of the world. Manifestation is surely an important part of the individual pursuit of happiness, but it is most powerful when it is aligned with the collective pursuit of benevolence and our need to support one another.

When doing manifestation work, it is important to make a crucial distinction between profit and prosperity. Generating profit is often seen in terms of profiting at someone else's loss—a matter of buying low and selling high. Abundant manifestation occurs when the sense of prosperity is all-inclusive—you do not seek to profit at someone else's expense, but rather, in the pursuit of service to others, you find all you need to accomplish the task at hand, and more.

In terms of our work in the world, one of the most important things you can do as you fill out your manifestation lists and build your mandala, is to examine the areas in which you are currently ready to make a contribution to your cultural environment. Beginning to think in this way is a tool to weave together your personal vocation and job satisfaction with a greater sense of culture, history, and your place in your community. This is the key to deepening your sense of manifestation until it reflects a renewed sense of alignment and nobility. In this understanding of abundance, it is important not to leave anything or anyone behind. The issue here is not only about work or vocation in terms of what you are supposed to do, but about an evolving work ethic that supports an enlightened age and enlightened people.

The Alchemy of Abundance includes a deep understanding of the myriad forms in which we exchange goods, services, information, and imagery. This deepened understanding of the different facets of "capital" makes clear that personal growth and spirituality never exist within an economic vacuum. For instance, many people may feel trapped in an unsatisfactory work situation when they are in debt or feel that they cannot leave their current employment because they are dependent upon employer-supplied health care for their family. This kind of entrapment also occurs when a business becomes exclusively market driven as opposed to values driven. Company owners will feel similar pressures—they do not have the freedom to be creative or innovative because they are dependent on the present market.

From the point of view of the Alchemy of Abundance, the most important factor that can assist us in the pursuit of balance is the triumph of principle: allow the market to align with your values, power, and integrity. Do not sacrifice your God-given abundance and well-being. This takes us back to the very beginning of the program when I asked you to define abundance and well-being for yourself. What is the "good life," really? The challenge here is to articulate the values that are so essential and true that they send shivers through your body. For me, abundance by definition leaves out no animal, no plant, nobody—including those not yet born who have entrusted us with their future on this planet.

Sripad Baba, the mysterious Tantric adept from Vrindaban, India, used to say, "Awareness is not sustained by effort; it is sustained by grace." Part of the practice of abundance may be a return to grace in a new way. Perhaps we no longer need to lose everything and become destitute and forlorn like Job in order to experience God's grace. A more compassionate image of grace may be that of the Divine Mother who loves all of her children and wants nothing but the best for them. Perhaps we can learn how to receive the bounty and goodness of the most beautiful things in life and still be open to the realities of impermanence and disillusion. Is it really suffering that is being asked of us, or are we being asked to open to the full cycle of the human experience with an attitude of gratitude and understanding? Can we learn to allow these gifts that arise out of the miraculous, to come to us gracefully, and then just as gracefully let them go back to where they came from?

A while back when my daughter was four years old, a friend of hers' asked, "Are you Christian; do you celebrate Christmas?" She responded with a cute, long, drawn-out, "Nooo." So she asked her, "Are you Jewish; do you celebrate Hanukkah?" She again said "Nooo." "Well," she said, "What are you?" My daughter then replied, "I am happy." This happiness is the grace of manifestation in our daily life. By opening to the mystery of the juxtaposition of the ordinary and the extraordinary, we can learn to live the Alchemy of Abundance, while still being Christian, Jewish, Islamic, Buddhist, Hindu, Taoist, Pagan, Secular, or whatever we are meant to be. We can allow ourselves to be broken open by the mysteries of life and to express this practice of openness with others, which is true compassion. To be fully abundant is to be able to let go of anxiety, knowing that everything we need is ever-woven into the fabric of existence that surrounds and supports us at every moment through the open-armed grace of the ever-present Beloved One.

RETURNING TO YOUR BEGINNING

Go back to your first entry in your journal, where you defined abundance for yourself. Have your definitions and understandings changed in any way? Allow yourself to articulate what abundance means to you now, and let it continue to evolve. Likewise, practice grounding your felt abundance by constantly clarifying and focusing on what you want, on what is important for you and your community.

The final mantra in the practice of abundance is this: "Finish it." Whatever you have started, bring it to completion; whatever you have taken in, digest it. There is a reason that you purchased this program. It has to do with your deepest hopes, dreams, visions, intentions, and understandings that inherently resonated with this material. Honor them—this is how your abundance is activated and this will maintain the passion that brought you to this work and will support you on your way as you assimilate it. Take what you need and make it your own. As you go on your way, you can be assured that your pursuit of alignment will not only bring you to your right place at the right time, it will bring you in touch with the communities of souls who have dedicated themselves to the renewal of the Earth, to their shared visions of hope, and to their brilliant flames of love.

About the Author

RICK JAROW, PH.D. is a practicing alternative career counselor, an Associate Professor of religious studies at Vassar College, and author of *Creating the Work You Love: Courage, Commitment, and Career; In Search of the Sacred: A Pilgrimage to Holy Places;* and more. His acclaimed national seminars, based upon years of research and practice with lineage holders in both Eastern and Western traditions, focus on interfacing intuitive inner experience with effective action in the world. For more information on Rick Jarow and his work, please visit www.anticareer.com.

CD SESSIONS